National Wildlife Refuges of Alaska
·Wild Wonders–Wild Lands·

By Elaine Rhode

Table of Contents

Encompasses public lands in the coastal
waters and adjacent seas (except Beaufort Sea)
of Alaska consisting of islands, islets, rocks, reefs, capes, and spires.

CHUKCHI SEA

NORTON SOU

NUNIVAK ISLAND

KUSKOKWIM BAY

PRIBILOF ISLANDS

ARCTIC OCEAN

COLVILLE RIVER

NOATAK RIVER

KOBUK RIVER

KONUKUK RIVER

YUKON RIVER

YUKON RIVER

NOWITNA RIVER

FAIRBANKS

TANANA RIVER

MT. McKINLEY

SUSITNA RIVER

KUSKOKWIM RIVER

COPPER RIVER

ANCHORAGE

NUSHAGAK RIVER

HOMER

GULF OF ALASKA

BAY

Kenai
National Wildlife Refuge
24

Tetlin National
Wildlife Refuge
42

JUNEAU

SITKA

Kodiak
National Wildlife Refuge
30

PACIFIC OCEAN

Photography Credits

(F = full page, U = upper part of page, M = middle part of page, L – lower part of page, UR = upper on right, UL = upper on left, LR = lower on right, LL = lower on left)

Michael DeYoung: 27L
Mark Emery: front cover, 12L, 16, 17U, 17L, 23L, 25F, 29U, 29L, 31F, 31U, 31L, 33, 34-35, 35U, 36, 37U, 41U, 45U, 45L, 48F, 48U, 48L, 49M, 52U
Laura Greffenius: 47U
Fred Hirschman: 47F, 49U
Karen Jettmar: 11F, 12F
Gary Kramer: 19U
Steven Kazlowski: 27U
Joe Meehan: 5U, 6L, 32F, 32U
Yva Momatiuk and John Eastcott: 3F
Ron Niebrugge: inside front/back cover
Jo Overholt: 37L
Gary Schultz: 11U, 11L
Ken Whitten: 39M

United States Fish and Wildlife Service:
7, 18, 19M, 21LR, 23F, 25L, 28-29, 43L, 44U, 56U, 57
Ed Bailey: 4
Ted Bailey: opposite page, 25U, 28L
Mark Bertrum 55M
Tim Bowman: 8, 14U, 21UL, 53UR
Vern Byrd: 6U
Donna Dewhurst: 9F, 9U, 9L, 17M, 37M
Lisa Haggblom: title Page, 46, 47L
Patricia J. Heglund: 55L, 56F
Leslie Kerr: 19L, 21UR, 30, 34L, 35L, 41F, 41L
D. Kildaw: 3U
Marc Lester/Anchorage Daily News: 55U
Vivian Mendenhall: 39L, 43U
C. Schlawe: 5L
Scott Schliebe: 14-15, 15L
Art Sowls: 2
Hank Timm: 26
Larry Vanderlinden: 23U, 44F

United States Geological Survey: 43F
Craig Ely: 13L, 51U, 52F
Robert E. Gill: 13U, 51F, 51L, 53UL
Jeff Pelayo: 39U
Dave Ward: 21LL

Printed in Hong Kong on recycled paper.

Acknowledgements

The seed for this book was planted in all the field camps I have worked throughout Alaska – from Prince William Sound to Buldir and Attu in the Aleutian Islands to the Seward Peninsula and the Arctic Coast. Whether I was documenting muskoxen leaving the Yukon Delta Refuge for Russia, floating wild rivers near Selawik and on the Yukon Flats refuges, or counting duck broods along the Innoko River, I learned from the land and its wildlife.

And all along the way, I learned from dedicated men and women working in and for Alaska's national wildlife refuges who shared their time and years of knowledge. I thank them for their generous help in the preparation of this book and – most of all – for their passionate support of this nation's wild resources.

– Elaine Rhode

Elaine Rhode came to Alaska in 1972 to help propose new and expanded national wildlife refuges authorized under the Alaska Native Claims Settlement Act. Her work and play took her around the coast and throughout the state's interior by small aircraft, survey boat, canoe, and on foot – tutored by some of the finest people dedicated to wildlife and their wild lands. She lives in Anchorage where she writes and edits.

Designer: Chris Byrd
Author/Editor: Elaine Rhode
Project Manager: Lisa Oakley
Agency Coordinator: Cathy Rezabeck

750 West Second Avenue, Suite 100
Anchorage, AK 99501
www.alaskanha.org

Alaska Natural History Association is a nonprofit publisher of books and other materials about Alaska's public lands. For more information or to join: **www.alaskanha.org**

ISBN: 0-930931-55-6

Library of Congress Cataloging-in-Publication Data

Rhode, Elaine.
Wild wonders, wild lands : national wildlife refuges of Alaska / by Elaine Rhode.
p. cm.
Includes bibliographical references (p.).
ISBN 0-930931-55-6 (pbk.)
1. Wildlife refuges-Alaska. I. Title.
QL84.22.A4R46 2003
508.798--dc22
2003019618

Wild Wonders

It's early April and life quickens on the wild lands of Alaska's national wildlife refuges. The start of 24-hour sunshine above the Arctic Circle is more than a month away, but the lengthening days stir changes everywhere.

On the snowy expanse of the arctic coastal plain, in the lee of a stream bank, a snow drift bulges and cracks. Black nose and long white muzzle protrude, tasting the air. More snow slides away as the polar bear pushes her head free and looks around. It's a world she hasn't seen since November when she tunneled into this drift to carve her maternity den. Her twin cubs, born in December, will remain unaware of the outside world for few more days until she acclimates, stretches, and digs through the snow to eat greens to restart her system.

About 700 miles southwest, a feeding flock of ptarmigan looks like snowy bumps on the uneven tundra. They still wear winter white feathers from head to between their toes. Flying low, a gyrfalcon zooms toward them. Bam. Half the flock explodes into flight. He carries his courtship offering to a distant cliff where a large female gyrfalcon is inspecting a selection of stick nests built by ravens and golden eagles.

Throughout the state, caribou are on the move. Pregnant cows, still with antlers, separate themselves from the herd on its more sheltered winter territory. Joined by some yearlings, they are the first to drift toward their herd's traditional calving grounds, perhaps hundreds of miles away. Bulls will follow several weeks later.

In the ocean, salmon are swimming back toward Alaska after growing for one to five years at sea. If fishing nets, anglers, or brown bears don't catch them, they will return unerringly to spawn and die in the streams where they hatched. The larval fishes from last year's spawning are consuming their yolk sacs and will be ready to emerge from their gravel nests as the ice goes out on the rivers.

In the air – from Antarctica, Australia, Asia, South America, and the rest of North America – migratory birds are flying toward Alaska. Geese, ducks, swans, and sandhill cranes will be the first to arrive even before the snow leaves the ground or all lakes and rivers are ice-free. These birds fly thousands of miles, bypassing other areas, to nest and raise their young on Alaska's national wildlife refuges.

Wild Lands

Those wild wonders – the denning polar bear and her cubs, the courting gyrfalcons, the migrating caribou, salmon, and waterfowl – are part of the daily rhythms of life on the 16 national wildlife refuges in Alaska. The refuges are guardians of the wild lands that the animals require to keep that rhythm beating for future generations to hear.

Wildlife thrive here, defying the Far North's reputation as harsh and barren. Of those that live here year-round, many could live nowhere else. Undisturbed open space with room to roam is one of their key habitat requirements. Alaska's multitude of sea-run and freshwater fish would shrink to few without the miles of cold, clean, free-running streams and lakes for their eggs. Sheefish even wait to spawn until the river temperatures drop near freezing in late fall. Nearly one hundred million migratory birds find maternity and banquet accommodations. They take advantage of the long daylight to feed around-the-clock, jump-starting their newly hatched young on a food supply so abundant that it makes the extra flight miles worth the trip.

The lands that support such abundance are part of a national network of more than 540 refuges managed by the U.S. Fish and Wildlife Service and dedicated to conserve and protect wildlife and their habitats.

Refuges in the other 49 states and two territories do their best to protect fragments of habitat and many must repair and restore even those. In Alaska entire ecological regions remain intact and wild. The food webs are unbroken and large mammals continue to move freely across the landscape as they have for ages. The challenge here in Alaska is to maintain these environments in their natural working order.

Animals benefit and so do we – Alaska's refuges meet our needs too.

Spawning rivers on Alaska's refuges produce some of the largest runs of wild salmon for the world to eat. Descendants of Alaska's First Peoples continue to fish, hunt, and gather on these lands to nourish their cultural traditions as well as their bodies. All Alaskans and visitors can enjoy the bounties of these lands whether they are fishing, hunting, wildlife viewing, hiking, camping, boating, photographing, or finding wild solitude. And, in this increasingly urban society, even people who never set foot on the refuges savor the knowledge that such places exist.

Alaska Maritime
National Wildlife Refuge

Dense sea fog lifts to reveal rock cliffs soaring toward a summit still wrapped in its own cloud. Cormorants fly in single file toward the island. Puffins ride the waves then vanish in a flash of orange feet and open wings as they fly underwater in search of food. On the cliff faces, tens of thousands of penguin-like murres crowd the bare ledges while nests of kittiwakes cling to even narrower outcrops.

Near a rocky islet, a sea otter pup squeals for its mother who surfaces amid the kelp clutching green sea urchins to her chest. Farther offshore two teenage Steller sea lions snort and blow before diving.

Above a small beach, a brighter green mound of grasses hides the ancient remains of Native house pits. The hillsides are pock-marked with bomb craters, reminders of the only military campaign fought on American soil – and on a national wildlife refuge – during World War II.

Regions: Southeast to Arctic Alaska

Headquarters: Homer

Size: 3.5 million acres

Established: 1909

Wilderness Areas: 2.6 million acres

Access: Some areas by tour boats, aircraft, cruise ships, Alaska State Ferry

Facilities: Alaska Islands and Ocean Visitor Center in Homer

For detailed information, contact the refuge – see last page

Wild Almanac

Seabirds arrive: May

Peak times for Asiatic migrants: May and August

Kittiwake chicks hatch on the Chiswells: June

Ancient murrelets leave St. Lazaria: June

Steller sea lion pups born: June and July

Horned puffin chicks leave the Pribilofs: September

Sea otter pups born: year-round

Stretching from the southernmost part of Alaska to the Arctic Ocean, the Refuge protects breeding habitat for seabirds, marine mammals, and other wildlife on more than 2,500 isolated islands, spires, rocks, and coastal headlands. When overlaid on a map of the Lower 48 States, the Refuge extends from Georgia to California.

Thick-billed murres

More than half the land is National Wilderness Area. Only a handful of the sites are adjacent to communities, but that wasn't always so. More than 9,000 years ago marine mammals and birds fed and clothed Alaska's earliest coastal peoples and gave rise to prosperous nomadic civilizations. Today's Aleut/Unangan, Yup'ik, Inupiat, Dena'ina Athabascan, Alutiiq, Haida, and Tlingit all have roots here.

Refuge habitats are as varied as the cultures. Low, sandy barrier islands at the edge of the Arctic Ocean offer scattered driftwood and sparse beach grass for nesting black guillemots, common eiders, and arctic terns. Those islands contrast sharply with lush rainforests in Southeast Alaska and the active volcanoes of the Aleutian Islands. Together the Refuge units provide the only homes on land for more than 40 million marine birds and mammals that spend a majority of their lives somewhere out to sea.

The high cliffs of St. George Island in the Pribilofs shelter nearly 2 million nesting seabirds, including red-legged kittiwakes, a favorite of birdwatchers.

The islands ride the Pacific Ocean's "Ring of Fire" where earthquakes and volcanic eruptions sometimes form new wildlife habitat. (On the horizon: Cleveland, Herbert, and Carlisle volcanoes in the Islands of

Under cover of darkness

Odd, high-pitched laughter, rasping cries – and soft thuds – echo at night from St. Lazaria Island (15 miles west of Sitka). Storm-petrels and auklets return to the island under the cover of darkness to avoid hungry gulls and peregrine falcons. These nocturnal seabirds often smack into tree branches and tumble out of the air. They patter over the forest floor until they find the entrance to their burrows, dug in the soft earth, where deep inside their partners are sitting on eggs or their growing chicks await food. When these chicks are ready to go to sea, they too depart at night.

Rockslides and cliff ledges

Earthquakes and volcanic eruptions commonly shake Refuge lands, forming new habitat, especially in the Aleutian Islands. Crested and least auklets choose nest sites deep within rockslides or in crevices and chambers within lava flows. Morning and evening when mates exchange incubation duties, the sky above a colony fills with dense flocks of torpedo-shaped bodies and whirring wings as the tiny auklets dip, soar, circle, and wheel in unison before landing or going out to sea to feed.

Black and white tuxedoed murres don't hide underground or make nests. Instead, each pair lays a single pear-shaped egg on bare rock ledges of cliffs and stands wing to wing with other murres tending their eggs. When still unable to fly, murre chicks jump from their ledges to continue their growth at sea.

Dinner floating up!

The shape of the ocean floor near Refuge lands holds clues to why millions of breeding marine birds and mammals thrive

St. Lazaria Island in Southeast Alaska

Life-shaking events

The first Russian expedition to explore Alaska, lead by Vitus Bering in 1741, returned home with fine fur pelts from sea otters. The luxurious pelts started a 'fur rush' that led to the near extinction of sea otters, fur seals, and the Aleut people as well.

When sea otters became scarce, fur trappers dropped off pairs of foxes on islands, returning later to harvest their furs. By introducing foxes and (accidentally) rats to islands where native birds were defenseless against such land predators, humans effectively wiped out some ground-nesting birds and endangered others. The Refuge staff is still combating that legacy today.

World War II struck the Refuge on June 3, 1942, when Japanese forces swept into the Aleutians, bombing Dutch Harbor. They seized the Refuge islands of Kiska and Attu and took 42 Aleut villagers prisoner. Soon tens of thousands of men and machines swarmed over the Aleutian Islands in a 14-month campaign to recapture the Refuge lands. Lagoons were drained to build runways. Tent cities were dug into the tundra. And rats invaded more islands. The military remained after the war, later testing three nuclear bombs under Amchitka Island.

here. A floating banquet is served where tides rip between islands or the shallow continental shelf (less than 500 feet deep) drops suddenly to the ocean floor (6,000 feet or more). Currents tumble and rise, mixing and transporting a rich soup of nutrients into the upper layers to enrich marine food chains.

Reaching toward Asia

Many headlands and islands of the Refuge are the closest American land to Asia. The Aleutian Islands are crests of subterranean volcanoes that emerge like stepping stones in a 1,100-mile arc from mainland Alaska. East meets west in a melting pot of plant and animal life from two continents. Whiskered auklets, secretive and nocturnal, and red-legged kittiwakes nest only on the Refuge and off the Russian coast. Birds such as the Oriental cuckoo, Siberian rubythroat, and Mongolian plover migrate through here, some pioneering new territory and some blown off course by the frequent gale-force winds.

An awesome sight

The Pribilof Islands offer the best marine bird and mammal viewing from land. Their beaches echo with the roar of nearly a million northern fur seals and the soaring cliffs host more than two million seabirds. For viewing by sea, regularly scheduled boat tours to nearby Refuge islands leave from Homer, Seward, and Sitka. Charters are available in other communities near the Refuge.

Whiskered auklets are the rarest of the six auklet species on the Refuge.

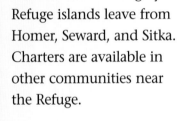

Northern fur seals, along with sea otters, were targets of early fur hunters.

6

Horned puffins gather on the cliffs, but nest within dark chambers in rock caves and crevices.

Alaska Peninsula
National Wildlife Refuge

Steam billows over the cratered top of Chiginagak volcano as the smell of sulfur arrives on a gust of wind. The earth is restless here. At the base of the 6,700-foot cone, more steam rises as hot springs bubble and seep onto the tundra. Come winter, the nearshore of Mother Goose Lake will not freeze nor will some ponds along upper Dog Salmon River, where buffleheads, tundra swans, and moose linger.

Notorious winds blow rain or snow sideways. Clouds and fog are normal; sun is an event to celebrate. Except along streams, plants survive by hugging the ground. Near the hot springs, however, bent and stubby cottonwood trees shimmer like a mirage. In their shelter, ferns and wild geraniums grow waist-high and lush. Like travelers to an oasis, tiny songbirds by the hundreds of thousands flock to this relic forest for a feeding frenzy as they fly between Alaska and Central America.

Region: Southwest Alaska

Headquarters: King Salmon
South Unit (Pavlof): Cold Bay

Size: 3.5 million acres

Established: 1980

Wilderness Area: 2.3 million acres

Access: (roadless) fly-in, boat, foot

Facilities: inter-agency visitor center in King Salmon

Summer temperatures: 65° to 35°F.

Winter temperatures: 30° to -15°F.

Solstice daylight hours: 6:53 in December; 17:42 in June

For detailed information, contact the refuge – see last page

Wild Almanac

Seabirds arrive: May

Spring migration (waterfowl and shorebirds): late March through early May

Spring migration (songbirds): mid-April to early June

Salmon spawn: July to end December

Fall bird migration: late July to October

Wintering waterfowl (emperor geese and sea ducks): October through March

Bears in their dens: November to late April

The Refuge stretches for 340 miles along the narrow finger of land that juts between the North Pacific Ocean and Bering Sea. From coast to coast, the variety of habitats form a huge oasis for wildlife.

Steller's, king, and common eiders find winter shelter in the narrow bays below the towering cliffs of the Pacific coast. Sea otters live

Black oystercatcher

offshore year-round, watched by black oystercatchers on the rocky beaches. Bald eagles, peregrine falcons, and seabirds nest on the cliffs. Seven active volcanoes rise along the mountainous Pacific coast. Mt. Veniaminof and Pavlof Volcano both have erupted more than a dozen times since 1780 and frequently vent steam and ash plumes. Caribou climb high onto Veniaminof's ice fields seeking relief from insects.

Below the mountains the tundra turns marshy, filled with ponds and meandering streams draining toward lagoons and the Bering Sea – ideal for migrating waterfowl and shorebirds. Marbled godwits nest on floating bogs, their only known breeding location in Alaska. Moose have been moving southward on the Refuge since the early 1900s. Despite the lack of forests, they find abundant willow shrubs along the many large lakes and streams.

Aleut/Alutiiq Elders say that when winters are warm, bears don't sleep well, so they get up early. Some brown bears don't den at all if food is plentiful. They can be seen fishing amid ice and snow in February.

Steam rises from vents on the shoulder of Chiginagak volcano, below.

Mother Goose Lake reflects Mount Chiginagak, one of seven active volcanoes within the Refuge. Ground-hugging flowers of moss campion and rock jasmine brighten the tundra.

Arctic *National Wildlife Refuge*

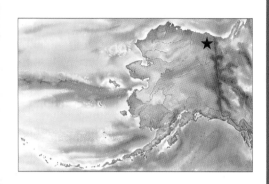

As the raven flies, a panorama of wild land stretches below. In the subarctic south, dark green spruce and splashes of birch and shrub willow signal the boreal or northernmost forest. As the land climbs farther north, trees struggle to survive and then give way to ground-hugging plants of the tundra. These foothills are home to Gwich'in Athabascan Indians.

Broad valleys narrow to canyons. Mountains, stacked 70-miles deep, soar to 9,000 feet with glaciers lodged in their crags. The massive jumble of the Brooks Range marks the continental divide where melting snow runs either to the Arctic Ocean or back toward the Yukon River and down to the Bering Sea.

Silvery rivers thread between the northern foothills and spill across the arctic coastal plain to the shore. For three months or less, open water of the Arctic Ocean laps the barrier islands and lagoons. This coast is home to Inupiat Eskimos.

Region: Northern Alaska

Headquarters: Fairbanks

Size: 19.3 million acres

Established: 1960

Wilderness Area: 8 million acres

Ivishak National Wild River: 60 miles

Sheenjek National Wild River: 155 miles

Wind National Wild River: 98 miles

Access: (roadless) fly-in, boat, foot, skis, snowmachine

Facilities: none

Summer temperatures: 75° to 25°F.

Winter temperatures: 0° to -60°F.

Solstice daylight hours: 0 hours from December 6 to January 6; 24 hours from May 25 to July 20

For detailed information, contact the refuge -- see last page

Wild Almanac

Snow: September through May (and anytime)

Muskox calves born: April and May

Spring bird migration: May to early June

Spring caribou migration: mid-April to late May

Caribou calves born: early June

Dall sheep lambs born: mid-May to mid-June

Snow geese staging: late August to mid-September

Pregnant polar bears den: mid-November to early April

The Arctic Refuge protects a continuum of wild environments on a scale last seen when blank spots remained on maps. Just hearing about these lands, seeing pictures, and perhaps – but not necessarily – setting foot on the Refuge can evoke a humbling sense of a world functioning on its own. By terms set down before humans arrived.

From the air, the land seems formidable, indestructible. From the ground, life's fragile hold is startling. Dwarf plants are cramped by permanently frozen ground and snowcover at least nine months of the year. They may form flower buds one year, bloom the next, and make seeds the following year – because their food supply and growing season are too short to do all in one.

Caribou on the move

Slow plant growth may be what keeps caribou constantly on the move and altering their routes. If bands of 10,000 animals fed every year or all season in one valley, they would not only empty that pantry but destroy it. Instead, they take mouthfuls as they walk elsewhere – and earn a reputation for being unpredictable.

Starting as a trickle, increasing to a tide of antlers and bodies, the Porcupine caribou herd migrates to calving grounds each spring from its wintering areas south of the continental divide

The valley of the Sheenjek National Wild River cuts southward from the Brooks Range, eventually joining the Yukon River and draining into the Bering Sea. The Okpilak River (left) flows north to the Arctic Ocean. Dwarf willow, only about two inches tall, emerging from snow (inset below).

in both Alaska and Canada. Pregnant cows lead the way. They head for the arctic coastal plain and foothills where fewer predators live and the plant growth is most nutritious. Calves born there are more likely to survive. By next year when young caribou return with the herd to the coastal plain, they will have logged about 2,700 miles on their life's perpetual journey.

Looking from on high

Mountains are the year-round realm of Dall sheep which means they have plenty of habitat within the Refuge. Ewes and rams use alpine valleys and windy ridges, always within scrambling distance of steep terrain for climbing out of reach of predators. They also climb to escape biting insects and heat, finding shade in rock crevices and caves. Bands of ewes and lambs feed and travel separately from groups of bachelor rams except for mating time in late November through mid-December. Dall sheep on the Refuge are at the northernmost edge of their range.

Snow geese

Autumn arrives as perhaps hundreds of thousands of lesser snow geese land in a feathery blizzard on the coastal tundra. They benefit from the isolation of the Refuge because they are nervous birds that take flight easily – and they have work to do. They've flown from nesting grounds in western Canada to find enough food to build fat reserves to fuel their next flight – 1,300 miles non-stop to another feeding ("staging") area in Alberta, Canada, enroute to wintering areas in the southern states and Mexico.

Ice walkers

When the geese depart and the returning sea ice chokes the offshore waters where bowhead whales migrate and long-tailed ducks gather, it's time for the ice walkers to appear. Polar bears, including many females and their cubs, prowl the shore looking for food. A number of pregnant bears come on land to den while others will den offshore on the ice. This is the only national wildlife refuge that hosts denning polar bears as well as brown and black bears.

Rescuing Ice Age Relics

The shaggy muskox, a relic mammal from the Ice Age, plods Alaska's tundra once again after an absence of almost 100 years. Their habit of facing danger head on, bunching in a tight defensive line or circle, usually worked to guard them from bears and wolves, but was no defense against spears or rifles. Overhunted and weakened by icy winters, they disappeared from Alaska by the late 1800s.

In the 1930s a small herd from Greenland was shipped to Alaska and released on the windswept tundra of Nunivak Island Refuge (now part of Yukon Delta Refuge) to serve as breeding stock to restore muskoxen to their former ranges in Alaska. The animals multiplied; and from that stock, two small herds were released on the Refuge coastal plain in 1969 and 1970. The herds grew and spread along the major rivers.

Less than five-feet tall, muskoxen are the largest mammal living year-round on the coastal plain of the Refuge. They endure polar blasts while wrapped in six-inch-thick wool (qiviut) coats covered by long windproof guard hairs. Their boxy frames also help to minimize heat loss. They conserve energy in winter by moving only short distances until June when the tundra plants turn green.

Wolf

14

Den sites for polar bears

More polar bears den on the Arctic Refuge than on any similar stretch of Alaska's coast. The pregnant females dig maternity dens in snow drifts on river banks or in the lee of bluffs. Insulated from the storms swirling above them, they give birth in December or January to single or twin cubs, weighing less than two pounds.

By the time the cubs leave the den in late March or early April, they weigh about 15 pounds. They acclimate near the den for up to 14 days, depending on weather, before moving with their mothers onto the sea ice. The family will stay together for two years, perhaps returning to scavenge along the shores of the Refuge next fall.

A polar bear breaks out of her maternity den in spring.

Bechar

Region: Southwest Alaska

Headquarters: King Salmon

Size: 1.2 million acres

Established: 1980

Wilderness Area: 500,000 acres

Access: (roadless) fly-in, boat, foot

Facilities: inter-agency visitor center in King Salmon

Summer temperatures: 80° to 45°F.

Winter temperatures: 40° to -40°F.

Solstice daylight hours: 6:24 in December; 18:15 in June

For detailed information, contact the refuge – see last page

Wild Almanac

Salmon young leave gravel nest: April and May

Emperor geese fly to nesting grounds: late April

Sandhill cranes arrive and bald eagles lay eggs: last week of April

Moose and caribou calves born: May

Salmon in rivers: mid-June through September

Sockeye salmon runs: late June through July

Peak fishing by bears: mid-July and August

Murres lay eggs in early July; chicks jump from ledges in late August

Tundra swans are flightless in early August

Songbirds depart early August to mid-September

16

National Wildlife Refuge

Willow shrubs and alders tangle the stream banks, mellowing the force of the incessant wind and sheltering hordes of mosquitoes. The stream ripples and boils. Hundreds of red salmon swim against the current, their noses guiding them to where they hatched four or five years earlier.

Around the next curve – splash. Grunt. A brown bear female stands in the water with two 2-year-old cubs. One cub, a dedicated angler, lands a salmon every few minutes, only to have them stolen by its sibling and occasionally by its mom.

Floating light as a leaf on a stream tumbling from one of the volcanoes, harlequin ducklings dart and bob, chasing insects. Their mother swims nearby, alert. Her feathers are a subdued brown, not the flash of blue, rust, and white of the male who left for the ocean weeks ago.

To spawn, salmon must survive a gauntlet of bears, fishing nets, and all the dangers of freshwater and ocean environments. From the thousands  of eggs laid by one adult, perhaps only three mature salmon will reach their home waters to spawn. Despite these odds, sockeye (red) salmon returning to Becharof Refuge produce the second largest run of their kind in the world.

The heart of sockeye habitat is Becharof Lake, an ancient earthquake scar 35 miles long by 15 miles wide and the third largest freshwater lake in the United States. The lake connects to Bristol Bay and is fed by two rivers and 14 major creeks, many coming from the slopes of the Becharof Wilderness Area. Chinook (king), coho (silver), pink, and chum salmon also spawn in these and other rivers on the refuge.

Salmon and the refuge ecosystem benefit. The returning fish carry gifts – minerals they accumulated during years in the ocean. Brown bears and scavengers are the first to benefit and recycle those nutrients. Red foxes, bald eagles, and wolves devour carcasses of spawned-out salmon. Any that they miss don't go to waste. Decomposing bodies fertilize the entire food web. Moose grow huge eating luxuriant stands of willow along shores and streams.

Native peoples knew the wildlife riches of Becharof long ago. Aleut, Alutiiq, and Yup'ik Eskimos traversed the Alaska Peninsula here, portaging between summer fish camps on Becharof Lake and the steep coast on the Gulf of Alaska where marine birds and mammals are abundant.

Salmon fuel the Refuge food web, from eggs and young to spawning adults (sockeye male, below) to spawned-out carcasses (left page).

Innoko

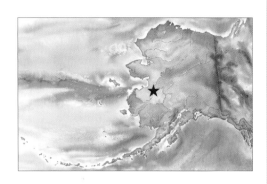

National Wildlife Refuge

Melting snow slides off the frozen land, testing the thirst of the Innoko and Iditarod rivers. Cakes of ice jam in the twisting bends and choke the flow. Water rises and spreads like a lake over the land, obscuring ribbons of meandering channels, oxbows, marshes, and ponds. Patches of forest become islands.

Robin-like chirps echo over the watery scene all day. But these singers wear fur. Yellow-cheeked voles, talkative mouse-like centers of the food web, climb trees until floodwaters leave their underground burrows.

Greater white-fronted geese and sandhill cranes, among the first migrants to return, proclaim nesting territories on the driest wetlands – raised bogs out of reach of the flooding and fed only by snowmelt and rain. Alert, the long-legged cranes stalk amid the tussocks. Stab! A wood frog just out of hibernation and hopping toward the bog, slides down the throat of the crane.

Region: Interior Alaska

Headquarters: South Unit - McGrath; North Unit (Kaiyuh Flats) - Galena

Size: 3.8 million acres

Established: 1980

Innoko Wilderness Area: 1.2 million acres

Access: (roadless) fly-in, boat, snowmachine, dog team, skis

Facilities: none

Summer temperatures: 80° to 30°F.

Winter temperatures: 10° to -60°F.

Solstice daylight hours: 4:43 in December; 20:18 in June

For detailed information, contact the refuge – see last page

Wild Almanac

Ice on rivers: mid-October until mid-May

Northern pike spawn: just after ice goes out

First migrating birds (geese): early May

Spring flooding: mid- to end May or later

Swallows arrive: late May to early June

Peak fire season: June and July

Birds begin leaving after young can fly: mid-July

Moose lie in rivers to escape insects: mid-July

Peak fall colors (yellow aspen): September

Snow: early October through end of April

Here on the Refuge, animals benefit from what would be called natural disasters in urban areas. Spring floods, coupled with summer lightning fires, work like gardeners clearing away old brush and fertilizing the soil for nutritious crops. Without periodic flooding, moose would lose the

growth of new willows that ensures their winter survival. Waterfowl would lose productive wetlands. Without fire, black spruce forests would dominate and provide homes for few species.

Every spring is different. In some years water rises so high that boats can sail overland. At least one old supply boat from the gold rush era lies mired in silt on the Refuge, caught too far upriver when floodwaters receded.

The lure of gold on tributaries of the Innoko and Iditarod rivers brought a wave of 1,500 newcomers to the area in 1907 and 1909. But like flood waters, they trickled away. The historic Iditarod winter overland trail, blazed to supply the boomtowns, passes through the eastern half of the Refuge. Today's Iditarod Trail Sled Dog Race uses a modernized route between current Athabascan villages north and south of the Refuge.

Before moose moved into the region in the 1900s, fish were the reliable year-round wild food for the local Athabascan Indians. They told explorers in the 1880s of the monster size of northern pike. Today the Innoko River watershed is known for its record pike, 55 inches and longer.

Sandhill cranes are among the first migratory birds to return to these flood-prone lowlands. Wood frogs emerging from hibernation become meals for cranes, wolves, foxes, and northern pike.

19

Izembek

National Wildlife Refuge

Region: Southwest Alaska

Headquarters: Cold Bay

Size: 311,000 acres

Established: 1960

Izembek Wilderness Area: 308,000 acres

Access: short local roads from Cold Bay, foot, boat, fly-in, Alaska State Ferry

Facilities: interpretive exhibits

Summer temperatures: 55° to 40°F.

Winter temperatures: 38° to 27°F.

Solstice daylight hours: 7:50 in December; 17:25 in June

For detailed information, contact the refuge – see last page

Wild Almanac

Steller's eiders return to molt (mid-August) **and depart:** late April

Ground squirrels hibernate: October to April

Peak migration of emperor geese, black brant: second and third weeks of April

Brown bears exit their winter dens (May); **first new cubs seen:** early June

Butterflies, bumblebees appear: June

Shorebird migration: July (western sandpipers) through October (dunlins)

Peak fall staging of waterfowl: September and October

Peak migration of caribou: November

Stinging, eye-watering northwest winds lash the golden meadow grasses. It's late September. Below the beach ridge, in the near expanse of Izembek Lagoon, thousands of black brant nibble slender strands of floating eelgrass, still bright green. Along the distant shore, an enormous brown bear ambles, fat rippling its glossy coat.

No trees, only volcanoes, break the skyline. A bald eagle stands sentinel on a nearby hummock watching the mob of feeding geese.

Suddenly, the eagle lifts off. The brant explode in a swirling mass of dark wings. Their frog-like croaks drown out the wail of the wind. Ignoring the commotion, a flock of mist-gray emperor geese continue to forage along the receding tideline, snowy heads of adults flashing brightly despite the overcast sky.

The smallest national wildlife refuge in Alaska occupies a place of giant importance for migrating birds. At the end of the Alaska Peninsula, with its shorelines facing both the North Pacific Ocean and the Bering Sea, this narrow 55-mile-long Refuge has some of the richest wetlands in the world. Dense growths of aquatic eelgrass in coastal lagoons and bays provide nursery habitat for young salmon and other fishes, crabs, and an abundance of invertebrates that in turn provide a substantial buffet for hungry travelers.

Flying from arctic and subarctic nesting grounds in Alaska, Canada, and Siberia, more than half a million geese, ducks, swans, and shorebirds arrive each fall, pausing to feed for several weeks enroute to winter destinations. Golden plovers and ruddy turnstones continue to the South Pacific. Semipalmated plovers and western sandpipers travel to South America.

Almost all of the world's Pacific black brant converge on Izembek Lagoon to gorge themselves on abundant eelgrass before their 3,000-mile flight over the ocean to Mexico. Brant will lose one-third of their weight in 54 hours of non-stop flying.

The only known wild, non-migratory group of tundra swans lives here year-round. When lakes on the Refuge freeze during harsh winters, the swans take advantage of thermal, spring-fed lagoons on neighboring Unimak Island, part of the Alaska Maritime National Wildlife Refuge. Many of the Steller's eiders in the threatened Pacific population gather here in August to molt their worn feathers for new ones. They will spend the winter locally in sheltered lagoons and bays before departing in April for nesting grounds in Russia and on Alaska's North Slope.

Almost all of the world's emperor geese (lower left) and Pacific black brant (center) stop here each spring and fall. Brant feed on eelgrass (lower right) in Izembek Lagoon (inset).

Kanuti *National Wildlife Refuge*

Snow falls like a whisper on the land ... revealing, not concealing. Tracks! Slide, hop, slide, hop. River otters search for food and a winter home near open water. At freeze-up, their tracks can extend for miles. Local people aren't far behind, setting trails for traplines or just enjoying easy travel after being village- or river-bound for months.

Temperatures soon can plunge to -70°F. The sun barely appears above the horizon, blending dawn into dusk with shifting colors of orange, pink, mauve, and blue as daylight hours shrink, then expand.

Circular paw tracks of a lynx meet the frantic zigzags of a snowshoe hare. Feathery prints reveal the wingspan of a ptarmigan taking off from its overnight burrow in the snow – a snow so dry that it flies up like crystalline dust. Athabascan Elders say if there are no fresh animal tracks, then it's too cold outside for humans.

Region: Interior Alaska

Headquarters: Fairbanks

Size: 1.4 million acres

Established: 1980

Wilderness Area: 500,000 acres

Access: (roadless) fly-in, boat, snowmachine, dog team, skis

Facilities: visitor orientation in Bettles

Summer temperatures: 95° to 40°F.

Winter temperatures: 30° to -70°F.

Solstice daylight hours: 2:10 in December; 24 hours from June 6 through July 7

For detailed information, contact the refuge – see last page

Wild Almanac

Peak northern lights: February through April

Geese arrive: late April to early May; some follow Koyukuk River to arctic coast

Songbirds arrive as mosquitoes hatch: late May

Last arriving songbird (flycatchers): mid June

Peak bear cubs, moose calves, beaver kits: June

Salmon spawning: early July to December

Birds start to flock, depart: late July

Greater white-fronted geese depart: end August

Beaver repair dams, lodges and cache branches for winter food: August and September

Ice: early October until early May

Snow is still on the ground, but retreating, as the first white-fronted and Canada geese, northern pintails, and sandhill cranes arrive in April. Soon an airborne flood of migratory birds, some from as far away as southern South America, reaches Kanuti Refuge and washes away the winter silence with a chorus of songs and calls almost 24 hours a day.

Ice leaves the rivers, and activities of wildlife and humans shift to the waterways, lakes, and wetlands that lace much of the Refuge. Rivers serve as pathways because overland travel in this wild, forested basin is tediously wet. *Kk'oonootne*, the old Koyukon Athabascan Indian name for the Kanuti River, roughly translates as either *"well traveled river by both man and animal"* or *"fish roe river."* Before summer ends, chum, coho, and chinook salmon will swim one thousand miles up the Yukon and Koyukuk rivers to spawn in Kanuti's streams.

Resident wildlife and migrant birds benefit from land saturated like a sponge. Moose receive nutritional boosts from aquatic plants that their winter diet of willow branches and bark can't supply. Awe-inspiring hordes of mosquitoes and other wetland insects and invertebrates feed tens of thousands of ducklings, goslings, shorebirds, and songbirds as well as countless fish of 16 species.

Beavers thrive here. The Koyukon Athabascans consider them one of Nature's great gifts: their tanned fur is warm, and their flesh tasty. Beavers create more ponds, stabilize water levels, and increase waterfowl and fish habitat with their dam building. Wolves prey on the beavers, often digging them out of their lodges in winter.

Winter transforms Kanuti's wetlands into solid pathways, making travel easier for animals and humans. River otter tracks can extend for miles.

Kenai *National Wildlife Refuge*

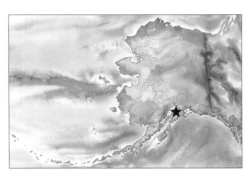

Region: Southcentral Alaska

Headquarters: Soldotna

Size: 1.9 million acres

Established: 1941

Wilderness Areas: 1.3 million acres

Access: Sterling Highway and interior roads, foot, boat, fly-in, horseback, skis, snowmachine

Facilities: visitor center in Soldotna, campgrounds, boat launch sites, interpretive trails, hiking trails, canoe trails, public use cabins

Summer temperatures: 80° to 40°F.

Winter temperatures: 30° to -30°F.

Solstice daylight hours: 5:50 in December; 18:55 in June

For detailed information, contact the refuge – see last page

Wild Almanac

Trumpeter swan migration: April and September

Caribou calves born: mid to late May

Moose calves born: late May

Mountain goat kids born: late May to early June

Peak wildflowers: third week of June in lowlands; mid-July in alpine

Peak sockeye salmon runs (two): third week of June and third week of July

Prime berries: early August for raspberries; late August for blueberries; mid- to late September for lowbush cranberries

---

Golden-leafed birches and aspen, illuminated as if by some inner light, blaze like torches against the dark green of neighboring spruce trees along the lake shore. The silvery splash of a rainbow trout ripples the mirrored perfection. Near the top of an old cottonwood tree a bulky mass proves to be the nest built by a pair of bald eagles. Empty now. An eaglet successfully took wing in August.

On the lake, floating among the curling lily pads, another family races the seasonal clock. Two gray cygnets, smaller than their trumpeter swan parents, must be ready to fly away soon, probably to the coast of Southeast Alaska where open water permits feeding all winter. Already a skim of ice rims the lake this crisp morning.

On the far shore, a bull moose breaks that skim with his muzzle and drinks deeply. His antlers are polished clean, ready for the rut. With luck, his offspring will drink from this lake next year

Early last century, concern spread that moose could disappear from the Kenai Peninsula due to overzealous trophy hunting. To ensure that moose always have a home here, President Franklin Roosevelt issued the order that created this Refuge in 1941.

Within the next three decades, wildfires burned almost half a million acres on the Refuge and gave moose the boost they needed to recover. Fire tends to open dense spruce forests to new sprouts of willow, aspen, and birch – food moose require to survive the winters. In old spruce forests, these can be missing or out of reach of even the tallest bulls.

At the end of last century great swaths of Refuge habitat again were altered. A tiny insect called the spruce bark beetle wiped out old spruce forests, boring under the bark and killing the largest trees. How moose and other animals respond to this changing environment will be seen in the coming decades.

Caribou goings and comings

Earlier in the last century a large mammal did disappear from the Kenai Peninsula. Fires and market hunters doomed the last of the caribou by 1912. Their winter foods, lichens, grow so slowly that, if burned, they take decades to replace. Now caribou roam the Refuge again. Two groups were transplanted here in the 1960s from the Nelchina herd in eastern Alaska. They wandered over the peninsula and eventually settled near the north and south ends of the Refuge.

Moose prompted designation of this Refuge last century because they were becoming scarce on the Kenai Peninsula.

Ear tufts help identify Alaska's only native cat. Lynx live in the forests near their chief prey, snowshoe hares. When the hares are abundant, so are the lynx.

Easily accessible refuge

Kenai is one of two national wildlife refuges in Alaska that can be reached by road. (Tetlin Refuge is the other.) The northern boundary lies just 15 miles across the waters of Turnagain Arm from Alaska's largest city. That's as the raven flies. By highway the Refuge is 110 miles south of Anchorage.

Good fishing then and now

More than a dozen Refuge campgrounds on the shores of the many lakes and rivers offer access to some of the finest fishing in the region. The Kenai and Russian rivers are renowned for their chinook (king), sockeye (red), and coho (silver) salmon, Dolly Varden, and rainbow trout. Ancestors of the Kenaitze Dena'ina Athabascans traditionally harvested fish here as well. Archaeological sites along the rivers date back several thousand years.

Trails into the country

Established hiking trails are unusual on Alaska's national wildlife refuges, but the Kenai Refuge offers more than a hundred miles of short and longer trails. They lead users deeper into the land for chances to observe wildlife and scenic vistas. The glacier-covered Kenai Mountain Range to the east contrasts with the lowlands sparkling with lakes and green with forests. On a clear day, three volcanoes – Spurr, Redoubt, and Illiamna – are visible across Cook Inlet to the west.

Undercover for millennia

Part of the Refuge will remain invisible, however. Mountain valleys and passes in the Kenai Range are buried under a jumble of glaciers that form the 60-mile-long Harding Ice Field. More snow falls here than melts, maintaining the glaciers. With icy teeth they continue to carve valleys, chewing up rock and spitting out silty rock flour into the rivers that flow across the Refuge.

Paddle into wilderness

As the most visited and accessible of all national wildlife refuges in Alaska, Kenai Refuge maintains more than half of its land in the National Wilderness Preservation System. Two easily accessible wilderness areas, laced with lakes, allow paddlers to enter the realm of loons, beaver, moose, bald eagles, trumpeter swans, and wolves. These Swanson River and Swan Lake canoe systems are designated national recreation trails.

Not to be confused

This is the only refuge where both mountain goats (above) and Dall sheep live. Nanny and billy mountain goats have short, spiky black horns and longer hair. Their realm is the steep rocky slopes and alpine meadows in the wilderness area between Skilak and Tustumena lakes. More numerous in the mountains of the Refuge, ewes and young Dall sheep have spiky brown horns. The horns of rams grow more massive and curling with age. Females and males of both species live separately almost all of the year, coming together only to mate.

Turquoise waters

The Kenai River runs a startling turquoise green as it enters the eastern edge of the Refuge along the Sterling Highway. The waters carry powdery rock "flour" pulverized by glaciers on the peaks separating the Kenai Peninsula from Prince William Sound. Fine particles in the water reflect blue-green light. The river then flows through Skilak Lake where the particles settle out – and the turquoise disappears.

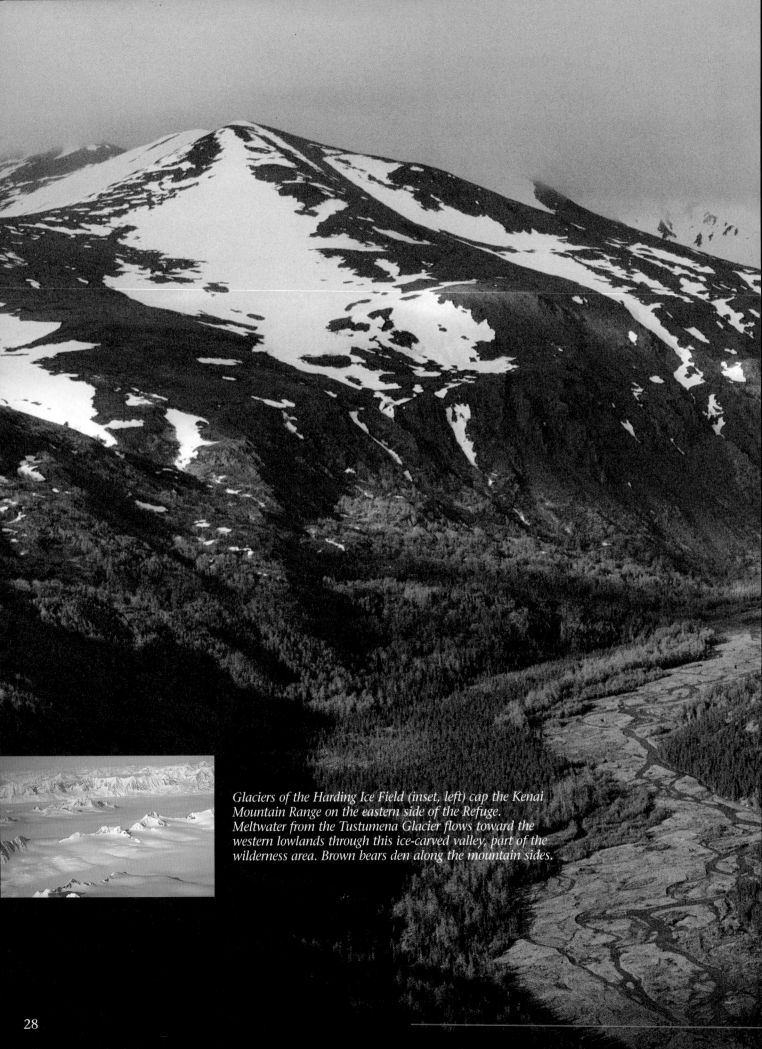

Glaciers of the Harding Ice Field (inset, left) cap the Kenai Mountain Range on the eastern side of the Refuge. Meltwater from the Tustumena Glacier flows toward the western lowlands through this ice-carved valley, part of the wilderness area. Brown bears den along the mountain sides.

Year-round importance

Visiting the Refuge doesn't stop at the end of summer. Autumn colors are spectacular for hikers, hunters, late-season anglers, and wildlife observers. Winter brings another magic, although some of the animals such as the brown and black bears disappear into their dens until spring. With its variety of wildlife and scenic landscapes, Kenai Refuge is a compact and easily accessible sample of far-flung Alaska in all seasons.

Kodiak *National Wildlife Refuge*

Region: Gulf of Alaska

Headquarters: Kodiak

Size: 1.9 million acres

Established: 1941

Access: (roadless) fly-in, boat, foot

Facilities: visitor center in Kodiak, public use cabins

Summer temperatures: 65° to 40°F.

Winter temperatures: 40° to 25°F.

Solstice daylight hours: 6:31 in December; 18:07 in June

For detailed information, contact the refuge – see last page

Wild Almanac

Driest time: late winter and mid-summer

Salmon in streams: mid May through December

Peak sockeye salmon spawning: July through September

Brown bears enter dens: late October to early January

Brown bears leave dens: early March to late May

Bald eagles nest: April to early August

Eaglets hatch: end May to early June

Salmon sway in the river's current. Some are silvery fresh from the ocean, heading farther upstream. Others are red-backed and ready to scrape a nest in the gravel to spawn. The scent of the water tells them this is the place where they hatched years earlier.

Brown bears, spaced at intervals along the grassy banks and in the water, study the flow and grab a meal as it swims by. A bear, fur glistening with mist and muzzle dripping river water, rises on her hind legs. She swivels her head, nostrils widening to test the wind. Three cubs freeze in their play and pop up beside her, imitating her behavior – learning to be wary bears.

Bald eagles watch the bears as well as the river, waiting to scavenge what the bears don't eat. They stand on the grassy banks and in the water, ignoring ravens and the cries of mooching gulls.

Imagine an 80-mile expanse of banquet table, continually refilling with the abundance of the season. Where a black-tailed doe and her fawn can pass unharmed between two families of dining brown bears because the bears are too full of salmon, greens, or berries. That's Kodiak Refuge.

Karluk River

The Refuge overlays the mountainous, fjord-cut southern two thirds of Kodiak Island, the second largest island in the United States. It also includes to the north Ban Island and portions of the rainforest of Afognak Island. The generosity of these lands are reflected in more than 8,000 years of settlement by Native Alaskans, ancestors of today's Alutiiq people. Land and marine birds and mammals were important in their culture as well as sources for food, clothing, and tools.

Before the Ice Age this island was connected to the Kenai Peninsula 40 miles to the north. Only six land mammals are native here: brown bear, red fox, river otter, short-tailed weasel, tundra vole, and little brown bat. Between 1920 and 1970 other mammals were introduced including beaver, mountain goat, and Sitka black-tailed deer (native to the coastal rainforests of Southeast Alaska). The deer were released in the spruce forests at the north end of the island and gradually moved south into the brush and tundra environment of the Refuge.

The most famous residents of Kodiak Refuge are the salmon that return to spawn and the brown bears that feast on them.

Abundant salmon in the summer and enough carrion to scavenge in the winter allows bald eagles to thrive and raise many eaglets. Nests are often on the ground as well as in trees.

Eagle opportunists

With few trees to shelter them during winters of deep snow, some of the introduced deer die. Bald eagles are quick to scavenge the carcasses. Winter is their lean time also. The population of eagles on the Refuge has grown to more than 600 breeding pairs.

Bald eagles nest near food – along the coast, on rocky outcrops or edges of banks, on beaver lodges, and wherever spruce and cottonwood trees grow along bays and rivers. They fish for a living. Chinook (king) and sockeye (red) salmon are returning to the streams as the birds incubate their eggs. The first salmon spawn as the chicks hatch.

Salmon make the system work

From May through December a parade of salmon fill Refuge streams and lakes. Chinook salmon arrive first, followed by sockeye, pink, chum, and coho (silver) and by steelhead (a sea-run trout). They hatched here but spent up to six years in the ocean where some gain at least a pound a month. When they return to spawn and die in freshwater, they share those supercharged marine nutrients with their land-based environment.

The salmon legacy radiates through the food web. Without the yearly banquet of millions of salmon, the land could not support the bears, eagles, and other wildlife that it does today. Even salmon benefit. When their eggs hatch next spring, the larval fish will feed on plankton nourished by minerals released from the rotting carcasses of their parents.

Ash fall and tsunami

The Refuge lies in a region of geologic hazards. Volcanic ash rained down on the island for three days in June of 1912 from an eruption about 50 miles away on the volcano-studded Alaska Peninsula. More than a foot of ash covered parts of the island and is still visible in the soil profile.

Earthquakes caused a tsunami (tidal wave) that in 1788 washed away much of the first Russian settlement on the island in Three Saints Bay. During the great 1964 Alaska earthquake, in addition to being hit by 60-foot waves from the tsunami, Refuge lands on the island dropped in elevation from one to four feet, flooding coastal areas.

Bountiful habitat, big bears

About 2,200 brown bears live on the Refuge, an amazing density of one bear per square mile in some areas such as Karluk Lake. While brown bears in the Arctic must roam across hundreds of square miles to find food, denning sites, and mates, Kodiak bears often meet their needs within a four- by five-mile area or less.

Kodiak brown bears are the largest bears in the world – males can stand 10-feet tall and weigh up to 1,500 pounds and females, 800 pounds. Twin and triplet cubs are common, another sign of a healthy habitat. Cubs remain with their mother for three years. Adult males are the greatest threat to cubs – they cannibalize them – so the sow is always on guard.

Bears break their winter's fast with carrion found on beaches or in the mountains and with large portions of roots and tender new shoots of green plants. When the salmon return to freshwater, bears move to favorite sites along streams and lakes for a high protein feast. As berries ripen and reach their highest sugar content, bears balance their diet with fruit of the thorny devil's club, elderberries, and salmonberries.

Uganik highlands – No place on the island is more than 15 miles from the ocean.

Brown bear cubs stay with their mother for up to three years.
They imitate her and thus learn how to survive.

O'Malley River is a favorite
fishing area of bears.

Koyukuk

National Wildlife Refuge

The low sun strikes the rippled surface of the Koyukuk River sending rays of evening light into the forest of birch and spruce above the bank. It's late August when nights become noticeable again after the endlessly circling sun of high summer.

The Zane Hills roll across the western horizon in fading layers, a traditional boundary between coastal Inupiat Eskimos and interior Koyukon Athabascans. There, historically, they put aside differences long enough to trade resources available only in the other's territory – seal oil and hides from the coast and beaver and fringed garments from this river valley.

Out of darkening shadows comes the hoot of a great-horned owl. Grass rustles. Hungry voles are scurrying along their hidden trails. On the gravel bar – movement. A red fox steps out of the willows, a spawned-out chum salmon in its mouth. Almost-grown pups back at the den will feast this night.

Region: Interior Alaska

Headquarters: Galena

Size: 3.5 million acres

Established: 1980

Wilderness Area: 400,000 acres

Access: (roadless) fly-in, boat, snowmachine, dog team

Summer temperatures: 90° to 35°F.

Winter temperatures: 20° to -70°F.

Solstice daylight hours: 3:04 in December; 24 hours from June 17 through June 27

For detailed information, contact the refuge – see last page

Wild Almanac

Bull moose shed antlers (December); **new antlers grow:** February until late August

Wolves mate (March); pups born in May

Foxes care for pups: April through September

White-fronted geese first to arrive: late April

Moose calves born: late May

Swan cygnets hatch: mid-June

Geese molt flight feathers: July 5-20

Chum salmon spawn: June through August

Ducks, geese, swan and cranes leave: late August through September

Ice: mid-October until mid-May

The Koyukuk flows leisurely southwest through the Refuge to meet the Yukon River. It bends back on itself in more than 200 oxbows, many now cut off from the main river to form oxbow lakes that warm quickly with the summer sun. Despite the short growing season, those lakes and adjoining wetlands are able to produce a banquet of aquatic plants and invertebrates. They feed thousands of ducks and geese that flock here to nest from all parts of the continent. Both the trumpeter and tundra swans raise their cygnets on the lakes.

The many bends in the river make ice jams common during spring breakup. Great slabs of ice climb the banks, snapping trees and gouging swaths clear of vegetation. This promotes new growth, a tender and nutritious feast for geese, moose, beavers, and snowshoe hares.

Moose are relative newcomers to the area, first appearing in 1900. They found untapped habitat that helped them expand and thrive. Twin moose calves are common, a sign of good food. Black bears are also abundant here, and they add extra pounds in the autumn by gorging on the blueberries that cover the lowlands.

Grinding with icy teeth, long-ago distant glaciers helped to form the Nogahabara Sand Dunes in the Koyukuk Wilderness Area. Although wind-blown sand and other glacial deposits underlie much of the Refuge, a six-mile-wide pile of dunes, some 200-feet high, remains starkly exposed.

Red fox and pups

Nogahabara Sand Dunes

Nowitna

National Wildlife Refuge

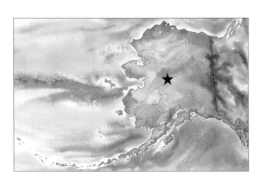

Region: Interior Alaska

Headquarters: Galena

Size: 1.6 million acres

Established: 1980

Nowitna Wild River: 223 miles

Access: (roadless) fly-in, boat, snowmachine, dog team

Facilities: none

Summer temperatures: 90° to 35°F.

Winter temperatures: 20° to -80°F.

Solstice daylight hours: 3:45 in December; 21:43 in June

For detailed information, contact the refuge – see last page

Wild Almanac

Rivers frozen: mid-October until mid-May

Bears in dens: early October through late April

Waterbirds return: late April to late May

Songbirds return: early May to early June

Marten (related to mink) mate: July and August

Marten kits born in dens: April or early May

Young marten hunting on their own: August

Lynx kittens born (May);
stay with mother until March

Snowshoe hares born: mid-May, late June, and August

Fog drapes the Nowitna lowlands and the surrounding hills as flock after flock of swans and sandhill cranes fly in formation through snow squalls and mist. A fleeting ray of sun spotlights deep tracks in the shrinking snowcover: a brown bear is out of its winter den and on the prowl. At the top of a spruce tree, a tiny ruby-crowned kinglet belts out its warbling trill, heralding the arrival of spring in the face of falling snow.

Each day more birds appear as more snow disappears. A single Lapland longspur is soon joined by a flock. Snow buntings, juncos, sparrows, and warblers – the migrants keep coming. Northern harriers swoop in courtship display as a flock of 800 cranes circles, rising on thermals billowing up from the valley. Koyukon Athabascan Indians traditionally taught the timing and sequence of migration by saying that songbirds arrive riding on the wings of cranes.

The first rush of songbirds to reach Nowitna Refuge spent their winter in southern Canada or the northern states. Neotropical birds flying from Central and South America will make up the next pulse of migrants – and include the splashy yellow Wilson's warbler and shy gray-cheeked thrush. Many only stop to rest. Others boldly sing to mark their breeding territory within a day of their arrival.

Spring snowmelt and breakup of ice on the Nowitna River often flood the lowland center of the Refuge, refilling sloughs and oxbow lakes and renewing their nutrient supplies. Carbonates flushed down from the limestone bedrock at the headwaters of the river help to neutralize the lakes' normal acidity and make them more productive than many others in Alaska.

By mid-summer, families of greater white-fronted and Canada geese will be feeding along the river banks as broods of American wigeon, mallards, northern pintails, and common goldeneye float with the gentle current.

In the spruce forest, martens chase red squirrels, leaping from branch to branch. Equally at home on the forest floor, martens also hunt snowshoe hares, lemmings, insects, and voles. Such small, unsung wildlife support the better known mammals such as lynx, wolverine, wolves, and black and brown bears. The combined weight of the small animals exceeds that of all larger mammals and birds that prey on them. The northern red-backed vole, weighing less than a candy bar, is probably the single most abundant mammal on Nowitna Refuge.

White-fronted geese and other birds migrate to this wetland basin from many other states and as far away as South America.

Sandhill Crane

Selawik
National Wildlife Refuge

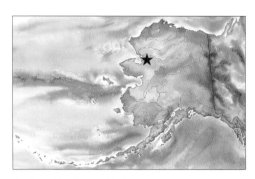

Snowflakes land with a 'hiss' on the dark, gently moving water. Steam, rising straight without a breeze, marks the course of open water for about two miles before winter at the Arctic Circle freezes the rest of this upper reach of the Selawik River despite the hot springs.

Moose trails crisscross the snow between willow shrubs, forest, and bedding sites in a patch of thermally heated, snow-free ground. Tap. Tap-tap. A three-toed woodpecker drums on a nearby spruce. On the hillside above, river otter tracks schuss straight toward open water.

In late winter as daylight lengthens, local Inupiat Eskimos and neighboring Koyukon Athabascan Indians from the Interior will meet here at the hot springs, in Selawik (Siilavingmiit) territory, and share the medicinal waters. Historically, their ancestors met occasionally at neutral trading places along the continental divide.

Region: Northwest Alaska

Headquarters: Kotzebue

Size: 2.1 million acres

Established: 1980

Wilderness Area: 240,000 acres

Selawik National Wild River: 155 miles

Access: (roadless) fly-in, boat, snowmachine, dog team

Facilities: inter-agency visitor information center in Kotzebue

Summer temperatures: 75° to 45°F.

Winter temperatures: 10° to -50°F.

Solstice daylight hours: 2:07 in December; 24 hours from June 5 through July 7

For detailed information, contact the refuge – see last page

Wild Almanac

Lemmings are active all winter under the snow

River otters pups born in dens in April; emerge two months later (must learn to swim)

Spotted seals follow fish up rivers in summer

Caribou migrate north (mid-March to mid-May) **and south:** September to early November

Geese from northern Alaska gather to feed before flying south: August and September

Sheefish spawn upriver late September to early October then return to the coast for winter

Sheefish eggs hatch: April

During winter, this stretch of river near the headwaters is the only open water on all of the Refuge. That doesn't stop village residents. One of their important winter activities is fishing through the ice for sheefish, some weighing 50 pounds.

The Inupiaq word for the Selawik River means *"place of sheefish."* This river and the neighboring Kobuk River are their only spawning areas in northwest Alaska. After wintering in brackish estuaries off the deltas, they migrate into the rivers to feed. In fall they move farther upstream to a nine-mile stretch where they hatched. Rising to the surface, spawning females scatter their eggs while males lurk below, fertilizing the eggs as they settle to the gravel bottom.

By this time the tundra has already turned its reds and golds, and the remaining blueberries and crowberries are frosted. The only likely observers of this mating ritual are moose browsing along the banks of the stream. Both moose and beavers began colonizing this region in the late 1940s from populations in Interior Alaska.

In contrast, a millennia of caribou trails cross the landscape. Sandwiched between ocean and the continental divide, the Refuge is a gathering place for the Western Arctic caribou herd each spring and fall on its perpetual journey to and from its calving area about 200 miles north. But, as Inupiat Elders say, "these caribou, you can't figure them." They often alter their routes and sometimes large bands will stay here in mild winters, feeding on lichens, undisturbed.

The Selawik River flows through the Refuge to the ocean, creating wetlands. In winter only a short stretch of open water remains at a hot springs near the river's source.

41

Tetlin *National Wildlife Refuge*

Region: Eastern Interior Alaska

Headquarters: Tok

Size: 700,000 acres

Established: 1980

Access: Alaska Highway, fly-in, boat, foot, snowmachine, dog team

Facilities: visitor center, 2 campgrounds, interpretive trails, 3 boat launch sites; no roads within the refuge

Summer temperatures: 80° to 40°F.

Winter temperatures: 30° to -70°F.

Solstice daylight hours: 4:34 in December; 20:31 in June

For detailed information, contact the refuge – see last page

Wild Almanac

Lakes thaw: mid- to end May (**rivers:** 2 to 3 weeks earlier)

Peak spring bird migration: last half of May

Peak flower bloom: June through mid-July

Peak blueberry picking: late July through mid-August

Peak fall colors: late August through early September

Peak fall bird migration: mid-September

Lakes freeze: late September to mid-October (**rivers:** one week later)

Snow: mid-October to late April

As the sun breaks through, fog and rain are forgotten in the wink of droplets reflecting a landscape turning from green to golden. New snow dusts the mountain tops. From somewhere in the western sky comes a faint, rattling call. Answered. Echoing louder. Brown dots against blue become flapping, gliding sandhill cranes. At first dozens, then hundreds and thousands in wave after wave of ragged V formations.

In the valley, brown and black bears rake through berry bushes with curving claws, scooping up more protection against the cold. Local people catch the urgency of the season and scatter to their favorite patches to gather cranberries, sweet roots, rose hips, and the last of the blueberries. The scent from a smoke house signals a successful hunt: strips of moose meat dry above an open fire the traditional Athabascan Indian way. All the while, cranes, swans, geese, and ducks are moving, stopping, moving again along the "Tetlin Passage."

The shift in weather that opens the floodgates of migration also brings Tetlin Refuge full circle. These birds are old friends. Many, now guiding young ones, stop here to rest and refuel each spring before flying onward to nesting grounds in Interior, Western, and Arctic Alaska. Some of the sandhill cranes cross into Siberia. For all of them the Refuge is a way station – a safety net – along their twice-yearly travel routes that may extend 5,000 miles each way.

Few birds can migrate non-stop. The majority fly in stages, following the retreating edge of winter. Birds that fly to Alaska and Siberia, however, must push their timing to be on site, ready to nest, as soon as snow melts and the short breeding season begins.

The Upper Tanana River Valley offers an oasis of early spring when all around is still locked in winter. The sheltering mountains that surround this lowland basin reflect the sun's warming rays and speed the breakup of many rivers, ponds, and lakes. In April migrating birds often wait here, feeding hungrily, until the next way station opens.

Not all fly onward. At least 115 kinds of wetland and forest birds stay to nest and raise their young, including trumpeter swans. These birds, shy of people, require privacy for parenthood and they find it in the Refuge's isolated lakes and ponds. Because of its location on the eastern edge of Alaska, the Refuge also hosts some birds that are rare or absent elsewhere in the state. Blue-winged teal, ruddy duck, American coot, sora, and red-winged blackbird – all warmer climate birds – are drawn to the cattail lakes in the warmest part of this valley.

Tetlin Refuge hosts one of the most rapidly growing populations of nesting trumpeter swans in Alaska.

43

Smoke billows above Trail Lake. Lightning strikes often ignite fires on the Refuge. They are allowed to burn when they would enhance wildlife habitat if no people or structures are endangered.

Summer clouds sometimes crack with lightning instead of rain, igniting wildfires. If the fires do not endanger people or buildings, they may be allowed to burn on the Refuge when they would improve wildlife habitat.

Fires return dense, old black spruce forests to mixtures of young spruce, birch, aspen, grasses, and willows – all used by a greater variety of wildlife. Fires also recycle minerals locked in trees and plants, fertilizing the next generation. New sprouts tend to be the most nutritious stage of plants and within easy reach of voles, snowshoe hares, and moose. Although a recently burned landscape may look bleak, the increased variety of habitats and the new growth that begins within days will provide better quality food and homes for wildlife.

Tetlin is one of two national wildlife refuges in Alaska that can be reached by road. (Kenai Refuge is the other.) World War II road builders connected Alaska to the rest of the continent via the Alaska - Canada "Alcan" Highway and chose a route similar to the one followed by migrating birds. Travelers entering or leaving the state on the modern Alaska Highway drive 65 miles along the Refuge's northern boundary. Fairbanks is 230 miles northwest; Anchorage is 350 miles southwest.

The highway cuts through a variety of habitats used as rest stops by birds along their migration route. Birdwatchers take advantage of the easy access of the road and the adjacent interpretive trails to follow the waves of winged travelers and see for themselves the roll call of birds that fly here.

Arctic grayling

Refuge campgrounds along the highway are near lakes with good fishing. During high summer, anglers even fish at midnight for arctic grayling, northern pike, and rainbow trout. Local Upper Tanana Athabascans favor the region's whitefish, pike, and burbot and harvest them for winter staples.

By the time temperatures sink to minus 50°F, the few birds that stay all year are fluffed against the cold and move only short distances, conserving energy. Then the caribou, always traveling, migrate between their summer and winter ranges through the Tetlin Passage.

Blueberry Lightning
Lightning strikes the Tetlin area so often in summer that it ranks among the most frequently hit sites in the state. Fires started by lightning help design the Refuge landscape and the boreal (northern) forest. When the flames leap and dance across the land, they burn everything to charcoal in one spot, but barely singe tree branches in another, creating a patchwork of old and new habitats that usually benefit wildlife.

Blueberries – the berry of choice of bears, voles, ptarmigan, and humans – sprout from existing roots left in the soil if the fire hasn't burned too deeply. Insects pollinate the tiny bell-like white flowers that precede the plump fruit.

Foresters estimate that almost all parts of the boreal forest burn at least once every 200 years in Alaska.

Togiak

National Wildlife Refuge

Below the cliff, hundreds of walruses doze in a mass snuggle on the beach. Other bachelor males are hauling their two-ton bodies out of the ocean to rest and warm themselves as they prepare to shed their old coats for new. The latest arrivals appear whitish. After days of deep diving, blood flow to their skin is reduced. The breeze carries their grunts and occasional bellows as they clamber over the others, flashing their long tusks to claim a prime location.

Murres, horned puffins, kittiwakes, and cormorants fly to and from nest sites on the cliff above the walruses. Mates take turns going out to sea to find food for their chicks. A red fox trots down the beach, following the scent trail of a brown bear that earlier fed on a seal.

Region: Southwest Alaska

Headquarters: Dillingham

Size: 4.1 million acres

Established: 1980 (incorporating Cape Newenham Refuge, 1969)

Wilderness Area: 2.3 million acres

Access: (roadless) fly-in, boat, foot; snowmachine, skis

Facilities: none

Summer temperatures: 70° to 40°F.

Winter temperatures: 40° to -20°F.

Solstice daylight hours: 6:05 in December; 18:36 in June

For detailed information, contact the refuge – see last page

Wild Almanac

Spring break-up: late April to May (rivers); June (for some lakes)

Peak bird migration: early May

Peak gray whale migration: mid-May

Walrus on beach: late April to late October

Salmon in rivers: May through December

Peak salmon spawning –
chinook and sockeye: July and August
chum: late July and August
pink: August, September (even-numbered years)
coho: late September to December

The Bering Sea of the North Pacific Ocean washes the 600-mile-long coast of Togiak Refuge and casts an important influence 100 miles inland to its glacier-carved peaks. The abundance of marine wildlife using the offshore waters attests to the richness of this ocean. Gray whales are common along the coast when they migrate between tropical and arctic waters. Steller sea lions come ashore in the greatest gathering of this endangered species in Bristol Bay. In all, at least 17 kinds of marine mammals frequent Togiak's coast.

Western sandpiper

So many shorebirds stop here during migration that their prime habitat, Nushagak Bay, was named as a link in the Western Hemisphere Shorebird Reserve Network which stretches from Alaska to South America.

Migrating black brant and emperor geese stop to feed at low tide along the shore or within the waving beds of eelgrass in protected bays and estuaries. An aquatic "field" of eelgrass is one of the most productive of nature's ecosystems. The eelgrass beds provide food and nursery areas for fishes, crabs, and many other invertebrates.

The ingredients that make the ocean environment bountiful also fuel the food web of inland Togiak. Marine nutrients literally body surf inland on wave after wave of silvery, sleek salmon. Tons of essential elements – nitrogen, phosphorus, carbon, and others – that salmon accumulate and store in their bodies while growing up in the ocean will be released when the salmon spawn, die, and decay.

Tufted puffin

Walruses grow fat and vigorous over the summer, feeding on clams on the ocean bottom and snoozing on protected beaches.

Salmon return from the ocean to the streams where they hatched to spawn the next generation. They must survive a gauntlet of hungry brown bears to successfully lay their eggs.

Each year more than one million chinook (king), sockeye (red), chum, pink, and coho (silver) salmon fuel this great nutrient cycle.

Everything benefits – from plankton and rainbow trout, to streamside willows, to humans. Some say that Togiak brown bears are actually 80 percent salmon. They can eat 30 to 40 salmon a day, putting on fat before retiring to their dens for the winter.

Salmon and the abundance they provide led some of the earliest Alaskans to settle here. Archaeological evidence suggests that some sites have been continuously occupied for at least 2,000 years. The Native peoples used resources of both sea and land and flourished because of the year-round diversity. In 1880, by one of the first censuses, more than 1,000 people lived in seven villages along the 60-mile-long Togiak River alone.

Today the local Native peoples are collectively known as Yup'ik Eskimos. They are the major residents of eight communities within or adjacent to the Refuge and many continue to depend on harvesting fish and other wild resources.

In a place without roads, rivers remain the natural corridors for travel – for fish, wildlife, local residents, and visitors. Fishing trips floating down rivers are the most popular recreational activity. The Kanektok, Goodnews, and Togiak rivers are the longest on the Refuge and start in the Togiak Wilderness Area. They flow swiftly but generally without white water. Sportfishing on these and other rivers lures anglers from around the world.

Many Dolly Varden, a close relative of the brook trout, are anadromous like salmon and move between saltwater and freshwater streams. But instead of dying after spawning, Dolly Varden spend the winter in fresh water and live to spawn again.

Seventeen other kinds of fish spend their entire lives in Refuge waters, including rainbow trout, arctic char, arctic grayling, northern pike, lake trout, Alaska blackfish, and several species of whitefish. Sport anglers who seek the rainbow trout owe some thanks for their experience to the salmon. Rainbow trout are as far west and north as they live, yet they thrive here because of the banquet table hosted by salmon.

Rivers of Livelihood

The clean, free-running streams of Togiak Refuge's 35 river systems are key to the commercial, cultural, and ecological livelihood of the region. All because they provide the right habitat to hatch and raise young salmon: gravel to shelter the eggs; cool, oxygen-rich water; and a constant flow to prevent drying or freezing. The carcasses of the adult salmon, in turn, power the food web that feeds their offspring and the environment.

Commercial fishing fleets in Bristol Bay and set-net fishers on the beaches await the return of salmon spawned in these and adjacent watersheds – nurseries to the world's largest sockeye salmon fishery. They harvest millions of dollars of salmon as well as herring from Togiak Bay and halibut from deep, offshore waters. These fisheries are essential to the economy of Southwest Alaska.

The Native Alaskan Yup'ik, whose ancestors settled here because of the abundance of fish, say that salmon are part of every fiber of their being. They dry the salmon to eat year-round, fish commercially for income, and some share their unique perspective with visitors.

49

Yukon Delta
National Wildlife Refuge

Region: Western Alaska

Headquarters: Bethel

Size: 19.2 million acres

Established: 1909

Andreafsky Wilderness Area: 1.3 million acres

Nunivak Island Wilderness Area: 600,000 acres

Andreafsky (and East Fork) Wild Rivers: 265 miles

Access: (roadless, many villages) fly-in, boat, snowmachine, dog team

Facilities: visitor center in Bethel

Summer temperatures: 65° to 40°F

Winter temperatures: 40° to -40°F

Solstice daylight hours: 5:36 in December; 19:09 in June

For detailed information, contact the refuge – see last page

Wild Almanac

Spring arrival of first geese: usually April 20

Spring arrival of shorebirds: late April through late May

First goslings: mid-June

First shorebird chicks: mid- to late June

Chinook salmon (adults) in the rivers: June to late July

Chum salmon (adults) in rivers: early June to August

Departure of geese: late September

Departure of shorebirds: mid-July to early October

The westward, rolling expanse of Alaska flattens here and, in a perpetual give-and-take with the Bering Sea, finally runs out of soil. For the last hundred miles, much of the land is less than 100 feet above sea level and frames one of nature's greatest collections of wetlands: large lakes and small lakes, ponds and potholes, trickles, creeks, sloughs, and Alaska's two mightiest rivers.

Amid all this water, surely fire seems unlikely. Yet come September along the coast, smoke rises, wafts, and dissolves. Other plumes erupt miles away. Not fire but tens of thousands of tiny shorebirds rising and wheeling in precision flight, their dark bodies suddenly disappearing in the flash of white underwing as they turn in unison.

Landing again on the mudflats, they race around, bumping into each other, all chattering. Their frenzy calms as they reestablish feeding space. Winds can be fierce out here, but sandpipers three inches from the ground keep probing for tiny clams. When their fuel gauge reaches "full" and the weather pattern is right, they rise in another billow of smoke and depart.

Flowing 1,955 miles from Canada to western Alaska, the Yukon River carves through canyon and flatland, forest and tundra before spilling its soil-laden waters into the Bering Sea. About 250 miles south along the coast, Alaska's second largest river (the Kuskokwim) drops its rich cargo. Over millennia these waters have been building a fan-shaped delta between the rivers' mouths.

Seals and beluga whales frequent the outer coast. In the rivers' mouths, millions of migrating salmon linger while their bodies adapt from freshwater to salt and back again when they return to spawn. People on the delta and up the Yukon and Kuskokwim drainages celebrate the return of migrating chinook (king) and chum salmon that give them both food and livelihood.

The delta with its maze of wetlands is the most important breeding area for geese in western North America. Shorebirds also top the scale, nesting in higher densities along the coastal zone than anywhere else on the continent.

Soon after the snow melts, millions of eggs lie cradled in clumps of marsh grass, scraped depressions, and on spongy tundra mats. Nests in the mountains of the Andreafsky Wilderness Area hold a majority of the world's bristle-thighed curlews. Coastal lowlands

Dunlin and other shorebirds bypass many habitats to fly thousands of miles to nest and raise their young in this rich delta environment.

The land cradles a nursery full of feathered young ones, including tundra swan cygnets

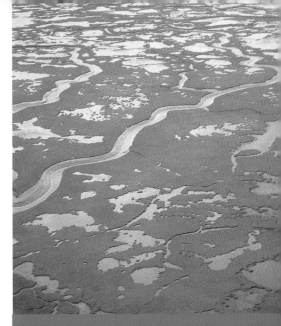

are nurseries for all of the world's cackling Canada geese, almost all emperor geese and black turnstones, and a majority of the Pacific greater white-fronted geese and black brant. The delta is the center for western sandpipers that alone number in the millions. Two threatened species, spectacled and Steller's eiders, nest here and spend the rest of the year on the ocean.

Sharp-tailed sandpipers

Many birds are international ambassadors. Sharp-tailed sandpipers, hatched only two months earlier in the Siberian arctic, fly east to the delta – without adults to guide them. Here they gobble calories for several weeks until their body-weight is half fat. Then they fly back across to Siberia and follow the Asian coastline down to Australia – non-stop, it seems, once they leave the Yukon Delta.

The importance of this area for waterbirds prompted President Theodore Roosevelt to designate the delta as the first national bird refuge on the mainland of Alaska in 1909.

Stretching from the sea to the mountains, the Yukon Delta Refuge is one of the largest refuges in the nation – about the size of South Carolina – and incorporates Nunivak, Clarence Rhode, and Hazen Bay refuges. Nunivak Island lies offshore from the delta about 20 miles. The island is volcanic in origin and has long been a year-round home of Cup'ik-speaking Eskimos and summer home for nearly a million cliff-nesting seabirds including puffins, murres, and kittiwakes. Muskoxen, brought to the island in the 1930s, serve as breeding stock to restore herds to their former ranges in arctic Alaska and Russia.

Ancestors of today's Yup'ik Eskimo residents found the delta to be a bountiful provider. People here eventually became the most numerous of early Alaska Native groups. Skillful harvesting and sharing of wild resources from fishing, hunting, trapping, and gathering remain the cornerstones of community life in the more than 40 villages within and adjacent to the Refuge.

Far from the delta, people on other continents are touched by the bounty of this Refuge. Millions of silvery salmon and winged migrants spread the surge of life nurtured here each summer.

Rivers in the Air

Waterways etch the landscape of the Yukon Delta, but they aren't the only paths flowing toward the Refuge. Birds in migration use "rivers in the air." Marked solely by the celestial and magnetic navigational aids in each bird's brain, these flyways connect the delta's nurseries and banquet tables with rest stops enroute from winter homes on five continents.

Tiny songbirds are the smallest navigators to the Refuge, often overshadowed by the more visible geese, swans, and shorebirds. Alder flycatcher, gray-cheeked thrush, blackpoll warbler, and northern waterthrush all winter in South America and nest in the forests and shrubs of the eastern highlands of the Refuge. The blackpoll warbler, less than six inches long with a nine-inch wingspan, flies nearly 7,000 miles each spring to raise its family in Alaska.

Some songbirds rarely found in North America migrate east from Siberia across the Bering Strait. The greatest variety of them nest in the north coastal part of the Refuge at Cape Romanzof. Red-throated pipit, white and yellow wagtails, northern wheatear, bluethroat, and arctic warbler brighten the tundra there.

Yukon Flats
National Wildlife Refuge

Region: Eastern Interior Alaska

Headquarters: Fairbanks

Size: 8.6 million acres

Established: 1980

Beaver Creek National Wild River: 16 miles

Access: (roadless) fly-in, boat, snowmachine, dog team

Facilities: none

Summer temperatures: 90° to 50°F.

Winter temperatures: 20° to -70°F.

Solstice daylight hours: 2:09 in December; 24 hours from June 5 to July 8

For detailed information, contact the refuge -- see last page

Wild Almanac

Yukon River frozen: mid-October to early May

Ravens begin to nest: end of March

Brown bears leave dens: early April

Pintails are the first ducks to arrive: late April

Black bears emerge from dens: late April

Ducks begin nesting: late May

Peak hatching of ducklings: early July

Peak salmon spawning: chinook (July) and two chum runs (July and August-September)

Sheefish spawn: early to mid-October

Bears enter dens: late September

A red-necked grebe slips into the water from her floating nest without a sound. Her mate, who weeks earlier noisily battled other birds to defend this territory, now quietly swims nearby. Suddenly there's movement on her back. Two tiny, black-and-white striped heads pop out from under her wing. A third chick jumps from the nest and skitters across the water to leap on its parent's back, disappearing momentarily in a fluffing of wings.

In another corner of the lake, day-care clusters of 60 scaup and white-winged scoter ducklings look like water bubbles as they pop to the surface then disappear, diving for tiny shrimp-like amphipods. One or two adults stay with the ducklings while other mothers take time-off.

After midnight, the sun brushes the northern horizon and shimmers on a pair of trumpeter swans, gently paddling, honking occasionally. Their cygnets follow closely. Splashes echo over the water as three black wolves trot single-file along the shore before fading into the shadows.

Soon after the Yukon River enters Alaska, it breaks free of confining mountains and flows for its next 300 miles through a flat basin about 100 miles wide, a place known for record high temperatures in summer and record lows in winter. Here, over millennia, the river's water and ice sculpted a masterpiece: more than 24,000 lakes and ponds and countless other wetlands that attract millions of migrating birds from four continents.

This wetland masterpiece is a work-in-progress. The Yukon River and 10 major waterways that join it here continue to change their channels, rearrange islands and gravel bars, cut off oxbow loops, pick up and drop loads of silt, and flood some dry sloughs. Fire, flood, and the intense 24-hour sun along the Arctic Circle combine to make these wetlands highly productive and one of the greatest waterfowl breeding areas in North America.

Wildfires sparked by summer lightning storms release carbon and other nutrients stored in trees and plants. Rivers often flood during spring breakup, redistributing those nutrients and other organic debris. If rainfall is scarce, by midsummer some ponds are dry and some lakes are low from evaporation. The sun's heat speeds decomposition of the exposed organic layers along former shorelines, again making nutrients available for use by the next generation of plants – and preparing a smorgasbord of wetlands to suit almost every kind of waterbird found in Alaska.

Marshes and lakes filling this flat basin provide red-necked grebes (above) and other waterbirds with ideal places for nesting and raising their young. White-winged scoters (inset) fly here from their winter home on the ocean.

The 24-hour summer sun brings record temperatures to the Yukon Flats and helps to make the lakes and wetlands more fertile. Food is plentiful for moose calves, but they must be wary of bears.

When drought scorches the prairie pothole country of Canada and the Lower 48 states, the Yukon Flats does double-duty as a safety net. Ducks that normally nest farther south will fly here. The unplanned extra distance exhausts their energy reserves for breeding, but they indeed find *refuge* amid these reliable wetlands until prairie conditions improve.

Some fishes rival the birds in their long-distance migration to the Yukon Flats. Sheefish and chinook (king), chum, and coho (silver) salmon swim 1,200 miles or more up the Yukon River to spawn here. Unlike salmon, sheefish spawn in only a few places in all of Alaska and one of their major egg-laying areas is on the Refuge, between Fort Yukon and Circle. Many of these large whitefish live to spawn again and swim down river to winter within the Innoko Refuge or in the estuaries of the Yukon Delta Refuge.

These and other fishes fed some of the earliest Alaskans. Chalkyitsik *(fish hooking place)*, one of seven villages here, began as a seasonal fishing camp as long as 6,000 years ago. Local Gwich'in and Koyukon Athabascan Indians continue to harvest fish as well as moose, caribou, bear, and waterfowl.

Moose are relative newcomers to the Yukon Flats, perhaps present only since 1800. In summer they can be found up to their bellies in marshy lakes feeding on aquatic plants. By fall – when the land becomes a mosaic of silver, green, gold, and red – moose move to the rivers where they find willow shrubs to carry them through the winter.

The Refuge's abundant black bears and its grizzlies (brown bears) are smaller than their coastal cousins and have short, barely five-month "growing seasons" before retiring to their dens. In spring, grizzlies sometimes dig out and eat black bear females and cubs asleep in maternity dens. During the summer, both grizzlies and black bears are the main predators on moose calves.

As lakes start to freeze in early October, loons and swans are the last waterbirds to migrate. Only 13 kinds of birds (including ravens, boreal chickadees, and spruce grouse) remain here in winter, along with furred and human residents. All the other birds that filled the forests and wetlands with their songs and chatter fly south, winged ambassadors of this and other national wildlife refuges in Alaska.

People and Ducks Versus a Dam

In the 1960s a hydroelectric dam project loomed over the Yukon Flats, ready to inundate seven local communities; the places where Athabascans and their ancestors fished, gathered, and hunted; and the breeding habitats for the animals they sought including ducks, bears, moose, sheefish, salmon, and countless others.

The Yukon River would be dammed at Rampart Canyon, just downstream from what is now the Refuge. After 20 years, the reservoir that filled behind the dam would be the size of Lake Erie. Although some said the dam would flood only a "vast swamp," the Native people, other Alaskans, and sport hunters and conservationists across the nation disagreed.

Biologists with the U.S. Fish and Wildlife Service studied the area's contributions to commercial and subsistence fisheries and to local and migratory wildlife populations. For birds alone, they found a fall flight of adults and their young numbered between 1 to 2 million from the area slated for flooding. Ducks migrated to as many as 46 states and as far south as Panama. When costs and potential economic losses were weighed against gains, the project failed. The area became the Yukon Flats National Wildlife Refuge in 1980.

For more information ....

**Alaska Maritime
National Wildlife Refuge**
95 Sterling Highway
Homer, Alaska 99603
(907) 235-6546
Fax (907) 235-7783
alaskamaritime@fws.gov
http://alaskamaritime.fws.gov
and
**Alaska Islands & Ocean
Visitor Center**
95 Sterling Highway
Homer, Alaska 99603
www.islandsandocean.org

**Alaska Peninsula
National Wildlife Refuge**
P.O. Box 277
King Salmon, Alaska 99613
(907) 246-3339
Fax (907) 246-6696
akpeninsula@fws.gov
http://alaskapeninsula.fws.gov
and
**King Salmon Inter-Agency
Visitor Center**
P.O. Box 298
King Salmon, AK 99613
(907) 246-4250, Fax (907) 246-8550

Arctic National Wildlife Refuge
101 12th Avenue, Room 236
Fairbanks, AK 99701
(800) 362-4546 or (907) 456-0250
Fax (907) 456-0428
arctic_refuge@fws.gov
http://arctic.fws.gov

Becharof National Wildlife Refuge
P.O. Box 277
King Salmon, Alaska 99613
(907) 246-3339
Fax (907) 246-6696
becharof@fws.gov
http://becharof.fws.gov
and
**King Salmon Inter-Agency
Visitor Center**
P.O. Box 298
King Salmon, AK 99613
(907) 246-4250, Fax (907) 246-8550

Innoko National Wildlife Refuge
P.O. Box 69
McGrath, AK 99627
(907) 524-3251
Fax (907) 524-3141
innoko@fws.gov
http://innoko.fws.gov

Izembek National Wildlife Refuge
P.O. Box 127
Cold Bay, AK 99571
(907) 532-2445
Fax (907) 532-2549
izembek@fws.gov
http://izembek.fws.gov

Kanuti National Wildlife Refuge
101 12th Avenue, Room 262
Fairbanks, Alaska 99701
(907) 456-0329
Fax (907) 456-0506
kanuti@fws.gov
http://kanuti.fws.gov

Kenai National Wildlife Refuge
P.O. Box 2139
Soldotna, AK 99669
(907) 262-7021
Fax (907) 262-3599
kenai@fws.gov
http://kenai.fws.gov

Kodiak National Wildlife Refuge
1390 Buskin River Road
Kodiak, AK 99615
(907) 487-2600
Fax (907) 487-2144
kodiak@fws.gov
http://kodiak.fws.gov

**Koyukuk National Wildlife Refuge
(and Northern Innoko Refuge)**
P.O. Box 287
Galena, AK 99741
(800) 656-1231 or (907) 656-1231
Fax (907) 656-1708
koyukuk@fws.gov
http://koyukuk.fws.gov

Nowitna National Wildlife Refuge
P.O. Box 287
Galena, AK 99741
(800) 656-1231 or (907) 656-1231
Fax (907) 656-1708
nowitna@fws.gov
http://nowitna.fws.gov

Selawik National Wildlife Refuge
P.O. Box 270
Kotzebue, AK 99752
(800) 492-8848 or (907) 442-3799
Fax (907) 442-3124
selawik@fws.gov
http://selawik.fws.gov

Tetlin National Wildlife Refuge
P.O. Box 779
Tok, Alaska 99780
(907) 883-5312
Fax (907) 883-5747
tetlin@fws.gov
http://tetlin.fws.gov

Togiak National Wildlife Refuge
P.O. Box 270
Dillingham, AK 99576
(800) 817-2538 or (907) 842-1063
Fax (907) 842-5402
togiak@fws.gov
http://togiak.fws.gov

**Yukon Delta
National Wildlife Refuge**
P.O. Box 346
Bethel, Alaska 99559
(800) 621-5804 or (907) 543-3151
Fax (907) 543-4413
yukondelta@fws.gov
http://yukondelta.fws.gov

**Yukon Flats
National Wildlife Refuge**
101 12th Avenue, Room 264
Fairbanks, Alaska 99701
(800) 531-0676 or (907) 456-0440
Fax (907) 456-0447
yukonflats@fws.gov
http://yukonflats.fws.gov